Legal Guide for Soldiers

United States Army

FM 27-14

LEGAL GUIDE FOR SOLDIERS

HEADQUARTERS

DEPARTMENT OF THE ARMY

Washington, DC, 16 April 1991

DISTRIBUTION RESTRICTION: Approved for public release; distribution is unlimited.

ISBN: 1490948236
ISBN-13: 978-1490948232

CONTENTS

PREFACE

This manual introduces you to the military legal office-- the office of the staff judge advocate. It also discusses the law as it affects you as a soldier in the United States Army.

Law in the Army does not deal with only crimes and punishments. In fact, only a few soldiers will ever undergo court-martial or appear before a disciplinary board. You might want to know about your right to take a job while off duty or to attend a political rally, however. You may need help with state or federal income tax returns, wish to be repaid for personal property damage while on duty, wish to have a will or power of attorney written, or wish to have some legal papers explained. This manual addresses many such questions.

This manual will not make you an expert in the law, and you should not use it to be your own lawyer. It does, however, address various areas of law so that you can recognize whether you have a problem and in what cases you should discuss it with an attorney at the staff judge advocate's office.

The proponent of this publication is The Judge Advocate General's School, US Army. Send comments and recommendations on DA Form 2028 (Recommended Changes to Publications and Blank Forms) directly to Commandant, The Judge Advocate General's School, US Army, ATTN: JAGS-ADA, Charlottesville, Virginia 22903-1781.

Unless this publication states otherwise, masculine nouns and pronouns do not refer exclusively to men.

CHAPTER ONE

Restrictions, Responsibilities, and Rights

Service in the armed forces carries with it a responsibility to the government and the American people that occasionally restricts your private and public activities. This chapter discusses how regulations restrict your freedom of action. It also presents ways to avoid conflicts between your personal interests and your responsibility to the Army and discusses your responsibilities as a citizen. Finally, it discusses the benefits that you have by virtue of military service, to include free legal advice under the Legal Assistance Program. Thus, this chapter deals with restrictions and responsibilities in the conduct of your personal affairs and your rights as a member of the military.

RESTRICTIONS

The following paragraphs address restrictions on your private activities.

SELLING TO OTHER SOLDIERS

You may work as a salesclerk in a retail store. Otherwise, you may not sell goods or services to other soldiers who are junior to you in grade, on or off post, in or out of uniform, and on or off duty. The sale of goods and services includes but is not limited to the sale of insurance, stocks, mutual funds, and real estate. However, you may sell your own personal property or home on a one-time basis to a junior soldier.

WORKING WHILE OFF DUTY

Off-duty employment, or moonlighting, is permissible if it does not interfere with official duties, does not bring discredit upon the Army, and does not violate basic ethical considerations.

For example, if you work late at a civilian job and then report for duty so tired that you cannot perform well, your job interferes with official duty. Working for a bookie is an example of an off-duty job that could discredit the Army. You must obtain written permission from your commander to work off duty for non-appropriated-fund activities on the installation. Examples of such activities include the post exchange, officers club, noncommissioned officers club, enlisted club, bowling alley, library, and rod-and-gun club. You may not work off post in areas where jobs are generally scarce and where your employment would deprive local civilians with the same job skills. Also, you may not accept employment with a civilian employer after the employer becomes involved in a strike. However, if you are already on the payroll when a strike begins, you may usually continue working.

SOLICITING GIFTS

You may not accept gifts from junior military or civilian personnel unless the gifts meet the following criteria:

- They are given voluntarily.
- They are worth $180 or less and have sentimental value to the recipient.
- They are given on a special occasion such as a marriage, illness, reassignment, or retirement.

ACCEPTING GRATUITIES

You may not accept gratuities from businessmen and private companies that either do or seek to do business with the Army or the Department of Defense. Exceptions include unsolicited advertising and promotional items that have a retail value of less than $10.

USING GOVERNMENT PROPERTY AND PERSONNEL

You may use government property only for official business. If you are going to school during off-duty time, for example, you may not use Army paper or an Army typewriter to prepare homework. This rule applies to all Army personnel. It is equally improper for a military superior to require junior soldiers to perform personal duties for him.

GAMBLING

You generally may not gamble while on government-owned or -controlled property or while on duty. Gambling includes lotteries, pools, games for money or property, and the sale or purchase of number slips or tickets. Some gambling activities, however, are allowed but only if specifically approved by Headquarters, Department of the Army. Before participating in any gambling activity on Army property or while on duty, you must ensure that the activity has proper approval from Headquarters, Department of the Army.

USING MILITARY TITLES

You may not use your rank, position in the Army, or membership in the Army to endorse any business or any business's product. For example, you may not appear in uniform in a television commercial to advertise for a local business such as a used car company. Nor may you appear in civilian clothes on a television commercial to advertise for a business and say that you are a soldier. Similarly, you may not allow a business to advertise using your name and rank. For example, a business may not advertise in a local newspaper that "SP4 Jones says he was very pleased with our company's product." Different rules apply to retired soldiers, however.

EXPRESSING PERSONAL VIEWS

You have the same basic rights as all citizens. However, many rights, including the most basic right of freedom of expression, are different for you as soldiers because of the need for discipline. American tradition requires that soldiers will not publicly dispute civilian leaders. Also, freedom of expression has limitations to prevent the public from attributing soldiers' views to the Department of the Army. For example, you may write letters to editors giving your views, but you should never identify yourself as speaking for the Army. You probably should not sign such letters with your military rank and title. You may write articles for publication but must get permission from your commander to publish articles on foreign policy, military matters, or operation of the national government.

PARTICIPATING IN POLITICAL ACTIVITIES

You may vote and express your opinions on politics privately and informally. You may attend political rallies and political club meetings and may even join political clubs, but you must never wear your uniform when participating in political activities. The reason is to prevent the public from incorrectly assuming that your participation represents the Army. You may not--

- Seek election to a political office.
- Campaign for a political candidate.
- Speak to political rallies or clubs.
- Hold office in political clubs.

DEMONSTRATING

Your uniformed attendance at a public demonstration may also give the appearance that the Army approves of or sponsors the demonstration. To preclude this appearance, you may participate only when you are off duty. You may not wear the Army uniform at any demonstration, and you may not--

- Attend a demonstration held on a military post.
- Attend a demonstration in a foreign country.
- Participate in a demonstration where law and order might be breached, such as traffic being blocked or police being assaulted.

DISTRIBUTING UNDERGROUND NEWSPAPERS

Underground newspapers are not prohibited if you produce them off post with your own time and money. Mere possession of an underground newspaper generally is not reason enough for the commander to take it from you. An installation commander may, however, require that you obtain his approval before you distribute underground newspapers on post. If the contents violate federal law, you may be disciplined for distributing them. You may not distribute a publication that presents a clear danger to loyalty, discipline, or morale or that interferes with the accomplishment of a military mission without the prior approval of the installation commander.

RESPONSIBILITIES

The following paragraphs discuss taxes and motor vehicle registration, which are your responsibilities as a citizen.

INCOME TAXES

You must comply with the income tax laws of your home state, or state of domicile. Regardless of whether your home state taxes your income, you are not required to pay taxes on your military pay to your duty state, or state of station, if it is different from your home state. You must, however, pay taxes on any nonmilitary income to both your home state and the state in which you earn the income. Your nonmilitary spouse may have to pay income taxes to both your home state and your duty state.

PERSONAL PROPERTY TAXES

You must pay personal property taxes on your solely owned personal property to only the home state. Although many states grant credit for personal property taxes paid to other states, property jointly owned by you and your spouse may be fully taxed by both your home state and your duty state. Personal property solely owned by your nonmilitary spouse may be taxed only in the state where it is. Real property is taxed by the state in which the property is located regardless of whether the owner is a soldier or a civilian.

MOTOR VEHICLE REGISTRATION

If you have registered or licensed your solely owned motor vehicle in your home state, you need not register the vehicle in your duty state. However, you may not avoid registration in your duty state by registering it in a third state that is neither your home state nor your duty state. You may be required to comply with the safety inspection and emission control laws of the state where the vehicle is registered, the state where the vehicle is located, or both.

RIGHTS

The following paragraphs address your rights as a military member.

REIMBURSEMENT FOR LOSSES

Congress has passed laws governing payment to you for losses as a result of your military service. Not all losses resulting from Army service are reimbursable. For example, a loss that is partly your fault is not reimbursable. Army judge advocates around the world process claims under the supervision of the US Army Claims Service. Army Regulation (AR) 27-20 covers the basic claims procedures.

Certifiable Claims

You may have a claim against the government if--

- Missing property is stolen from government quarters, from private quarters located outside the United States, or from an authorized storage place. Warehouses, offices, hospitals, baggage holding areas, and unit supply rooms are examples of authorized storage places.
- Property in government quarters or storage is damaged or destroyed by fire, flood, hurricane, theft, vandalism, or other unusual occurrences. Hail damage to an automobile parked on post and damage caused to property in the barracks when a water pipe breaks are examples of unusual occurrences.
- Property, including privately owned vehicles, is lost, damaged, or destroyed while transported or stored under government orders.
- Property is lost, damaged, or destroyed as a direct result of enemy action, riots directed against Americans overseas, soldiers giving first aid in a public disaster, and soldiers saving human lives or government property.
- Money is lost after being delivered to an authorized person as part of that person's official duties. Safekeeping in the unit and deposit in the Savings Deposit Program are examples.
- Property is lost or damaged due to wrongful or negligent acts of Army agents.

Claims Procedures

Although you have every right to file a valid claim, filing a false claim is a crime. You must be prepared to prove your damage or loss. Contact your unit claims officer when you believe you have a claim against the government.

If your unit does not have a unit claims officer, talk to the claims judge advocate at the post judge advocate office. Claims for less than $1,000 may be processed as small claims. Because this method is less formal, the investigating and processing may take only a short time. If you do not agree with the amount allowed on your claim, you have the right to a review.

LEGAL ASSISTANCE

When you discuss a problem with a legal assistance attorney, you create an attorney-client relationship. The attorney may not disclose information from his discussions with you without your consent or unless extraordinary circumstances exist involving criminal violation of the law.

The Army provides free legal advice and services to you and your family members on a number of issues. Following is a discussion of the most common of these.

Preparation of Wills

A legal assistance attorney may determine if you need a will, may prepare a new will, and may review your existing will to ensure it is up-to-date.

Powers of Attorney

Your spouse may use a power of attorney to clear government quarters, to ship the family car, or to cash your paycheck during your absence. Special powers of attorney are designed to confer limited authority for a short period and do not pose a great risk to you. However, general powers of attorney can be quite dangerous because they give great power and are difficult to revoke.

Family Matters

Legal assistance attorneys can provide guidance regarding the legal aspects of marriage and divorce. Chaplains, counselors, and Army community service representatives can help you and your family solve non-legal problems in these areas. If your marriage is not salvageable, the legal assistance attorney may advise you on separation and divorce. Help is also available at most offices on paternity matters, adoption, support obligations, and name changes.

Debts

Commanders may initiate administrative or disciplinary action against you if you fail to pay your just debts. Legal assistance attorneys can advise you and your family about the lawfulness of alleged debts and can help you decide what course of action to take. Army community service offices provide financial and budget counseling and can assist you in developing payment plans and budgeting schemes.

The Soldiers' and Sailors' Civil Relief Act (SSCRA) provides some relief with respect to loan interest rates and the payment of debts. The protection only applies, however, if the debt arose before your entry to active duty and your financial position is substantially worse since you entered the service. In the absence of a military draft or a reserve component call-up, few voluntarily enter the service if they will suffer serious financial harm. Consequently, few of those who voluntarily enter the Army will receive this type of protection from the SSCRA.

Civilian Matters

Army attorneys may represent you in civilian court to resolve your personal legal problems. For you to qualify, normal civilian legal fees must create a substantial financial hardship for you. Generally, married soldiers in the grades of E-4 and below and single soldiers in the grades of E-3 and below meet the requirements for financial hardship; soldiers in other pay grades may also qualify based on their circumstances. Any soldier may check with the legal assistance office to see if a court representation program is available at his installation. The legal assistance attorney may also be able to give you preliminary advice on civilian criminal matters.

Military Matters

In most cases, the legal assistance office does not defend you in military criminal matters and administrative separation actions. Instead, trial defense service attorneys help you with problems in these areas. At most installations, however, the legal assistance attorneys can provide advice concerning such administrative matters as liability under reports of survey and appeals of adverse evaluation reports.

Court Appearances

The SSCRA permits you, if you are unable to appear in court due to military service, to post-pone the proceedings until you can get leave. To obtain such a delay, you must have tried diligently to appear in court and must request a delay for the shortest reasonable time. Although attending court is often quite difficult during wartime, getting leave to attend during peacetime is typically not difficult. Judges are unlikely to grant you delays merely for your convenience.

ASSISTANCE WITH NONLEGAL PROBLEMS

Not all problems are legal problems. You should learn which command sections can help you find solutions. For example, the finance office handles pay problems, and the adjutant general's office processes promotion questions. Appendix A shows which offices can best help with specific problems.

Emergency Services

Several emergency services are available to you to handle crises. The Army Community Services Program provides information, assistance, and guidance to you and your dependents in meeting personal and family problems beyond the scope of your own resources and capabilities. It administers the Army's Family Advocacy Program, which seeks to promote a healthy family life for you and your family and to prevent spousal and child abuse. The Army emergency relief office can give interest-free loans and, in the case of extreme hardship, free cash grants to you and your dependents. The Red Cross can provide the following:

- Consultation on family and other personal problems.
- Financial assistance in certain emergency situations.
- Referrals to agencies that can assist in employment matters.
- Medical or psychiatric care.
- Children's welfare counseling.
- Emergency communication between you and your family when regular communication facilities are inadequate.

Emergency Leave or Compassionate Reassignment

Emergency leave and, in many cases, space-required transportation on military aircraft may be available in the event of a death in your immediate family or other urgent personal problems. You may qualify for a compassionate reassignment if you can show evidence that--

- An extreme family problem exists that you can solve only by reassignment and not by leave or correspondence.
- You can solve the problem within a reasonable period--usually one year.
- The problem did not exist or was not reasonably foreseeable at the time you last came on active duty.

In the case of both emergency leave and compassionate reassignment, the Red Cross will assist in getting information on conditions at your home. You should request emergency leave or compassionate reassignment from your unit commander.

CHAPTER TWO

Administrative Law

More than the Uniform Code of Military Justice (10 United States Code, §§801-940) affects your conduct and rights. Federal laws, Department of Defense directives, and Army regulations determine such matters as how claims are processed and paid, whether you can be discharged before your expiration term of service (ETS) date, and how you may submit complaints. This area is often referred to as administrative law because it deals with the administration of the Army. Discussion includes--

- Administrative separations.
- Non-punitive disciplinary measures.
- Conduct of investigations.
- Rights of soldiers.
- The limited-use policy of the alcohol and drug abuse prevention and control program.
- The complaint process.

ADMINISTRATIVE SEPARATIONS

Congress has given the Secretary of the Army very broad authority to provide for administrative separations. These separations, which are different from those by court martial, may be either involuntary or voluntary.

INVOLUNTARY SEPARATIONS

When you are considered unsuitable for further service in the Army or have engaged in misconduct that makes your continued service questionable, the unit commander may begin proceedings to separate you before your ETS date. The unit commander begins the process by forwarding a report stating his reasons for recommending separation, with all supporting documentation. Reasons for separating you involuntarily may include the following:

- Unsatisfactory performance.
- Misconduct.
- Other circumstances.

Unsatisfactory Performance

AR 635-200, Chapter 13, provides that you may be separated involuntarily because of unsatisfactory performance. It applies only to soldiers who have completed more than 180 days of continuous active duty. If you are separated for unsatisfactory performance, you will receive a general or honorable discharge certificate.

Misconduct

AR 635-200, Chapter 14, provides that you may be separated involuntarily for--

- Civilian court conviction as a juvenile offender or for having committed certain types of offenses after entering the Army.
- Commission of a serious offense.
- Abuse of illegal drugs.
- Acts or patterns of misconduct, such as repeated failure to pay valid debts, repeated failure to support dependents, or frequent incidents of misconduct with civil or military authorities.
- Minor military disciplinary infractions, such as disobedience of lawful orders, disrespect, failure to repair, or absence without leave. If you are separated under these provisions, you may receive a discharge under other than honorable conditions.

Other Circumstances

You may be involuntarily separated from the Army under other circumstances. The following chapters in AR 635-200 cover some of these:

- Chapter 5, Separation for Convenience of the Government (includes personality disorder and inability to carry out prescribed duties due to parenthood).
- Chapter 7, Fraudulent or Defective Enlistments and Inductions.
- Chapter 9, Alcohol or Other Drug Abuse Rehabilitation Failure.
- Chapter 11, Entry Level Performance and Conduct (applies to soldiers in the first 180 days of continuous active duty).
- Chapter 15, Separation for Homosexuality.

Any soldiers concerned in an involuntary separation will have an opportunity to consult with a military attorney. If applicable, you may request a hearing by a board of officers. If you request a separation board, the commander who has the authority to separate you will convene one. You have the following rights:

- You may appear before the board unless you are in civil confinement.
- You may request the appearance of available witnesses.
- You may request appointment of a military lawyer or choose a military lawyer yourself, but not both.
- You may hire a civilian attorney at your own expense if you desire.

The separation authority reviews the findings of the separation board and makes the final decision in the case. However, the decision may not be more severe than the action recommended by the board. (See AR 15-6 and AR 635-200.)

VOLUNTARY SEPARATIONS

Army regulations detail the procedures for granting separation from the Army before your normal end of service. Senior commanders or the Department of the Army reviews and acts upon these requests.

Dependency or Hardship

AR 635-200, Chapter 6, provides that you may request discharge or release from the Army for dependency or hardship. Dependency results from the death or disability of a member of your or your spouse's immediate family which causes the disabled member to rely upon you for principal care or support. Hardship results from a condition that involves the care or support of your family (not involving the death or disability of a family member). In either case, you must show that the condition arose or was aggravated excessively since your entry on active duty. The condition must be permanent, and you must have made every reasonable effort to alleviate it without success. You must also show the Army proof of the problem and proof of your need for release from the Army to correct it.

Conscientious Objection

You may apply for discharge from the Army for conscientious objection if, after entering the Army, you become opposed to all forms of war because of deeply held, sincere moral, ethical, or religious beliefs. An opposition to a particular war rather than to war in general is not sufficient for discharge. You may not request a discharge because of your conscientious objection before entering the Army if you failed to make it known before you enlisted. If you are opposed only to the bearing of arms, you are not qualified for discharge but may apply for classification as a noncombatant. Once so classified, you will be assigned duties that do not involve the bearing of arms.

Headquarters, Department of the Army, will make the final determination on all applications for discharge. Once you apply, a chaplain and psychiatrist will interview you. Then, an officer will hold a hearing. You may be present at the hearing, and you may ask the hearing officer to interview available witnesses. You may also have a civilian attorney assist at your own expense.

While the application is in process, you will continue to perform duties in the unit and participate in unit training. Every effort will be made to exempt you from duties that conflict with your stated beliefs.

Other reasons for voluntary discharge include the following:

- Separation for defective or unfulfilled enlistment or reenlistment agreements. (See AR 635-200, Chapter 7.)
- Separation of female soldiers because of pregnancy. (See AR 635-200, Chapter 8.)

- Separation for the good of the service when you are charged for certain crimes under the Uniform Code of Military Justice (UCMJ). (See AR 635-200, Chapter 10).

TYPES OF DISCHARGE

The separation authority decides what type of discharge you will receive based on your military record. If you are separated for administrative reasons other than for completion of term of service, you may receive an honorable, general, other-than-honorable, or entry level discharge.

Honorable Discharge

Issuance of an honorable discharge depends upon your proper military behavior and performance of duty. The separation authority may disregard isolated incidents of minor misconduct if, overall, your service record is good.

General Discharge Under Honorable Conditions

General discharges are appropriate for those whose military records are satisfactory but are not good enough to warrant honorable discharge. You may have had frequent non-judicial punishments or may have been a troublemaker, but your conduct has not warranted less than a general discharge.

Discharge Under Other Than Honorable Conditions

Only a general court-martial convening authority or general officer in command may give a discharge under other than honorable conditions. AR 635-200, Chapter 10, delegates that authority, in limited circumstances, to the special court-martial convening authority. Such a discharge will usually be given to those who have shown for example, one or more incidents of serious misconduct.

Discharge under other than honorable conditions is the most severe of the administrative discharges and may result in your loss of veterans' benefits, as determined by the Department of Veterans' Affairs. If you receive this type of discharge, you will not receive a discharge certificate.

Entry Level Separation

The separation authority will give you an entry level separation if you are within the first 180 days of continuous active duty and your records do not warrant a discharge under other than honorable conditions.

REVIEW BOARDS

If you have been separated from the Army, you may have your discharge reviewed by two boards established by Congress--the Army Discharge Review Board (ADRB) and the Army Board for Correction of Military Records (ABCMR).

Army Discharge Review Board

The ADRB will review any discharge, unless the discharge resulted from a general court martial. If the ADRB decides that the action was improper, it may change the type of discharge, but it may not revoke it and return you to active duty. If you want a review, you must request it within 15 years after the date of your discharge. (See AR 15-180.)

Army Board for Correction of Military Records

The ABCMR may review any discharge, and it may revoke an improper discharge and give a proper discharge in its place. It reports its findings and recommendations directly to the Secretary of the Army for final action. If your discharge is declared improper, you may receive back pay. The ABCMR does not return soldiers to active duty. You must request an ABCMR review within three years after you discover the claimed error or injustice, but the ABCMR may waive the time limitations when appropriate. Normally, applications for an upgraded discharge should go first to the ADRB. (See AR 15-185.)

NONPUNITIVE DISCIPLINARY MEASURES

The most familiar measures used in the military to enforce discipline and good order are the court-martial and UCMJ, Article 15. A commander, however, may opt for a variety of administrative actions in cases of poor duty performance or minor misconduct. Often these actions have a rehabilitative effect on you, benefiting both you and the Army.

WITHHOLDING OF PRIVILEGES

When necessary to maintain good order and discipline, the unit commander has the authority to withhold many privileges, such as the pass privilege. The unit commander does not have direct control over some privileges, such as use of post facilities and on-post driving. Only a higher commander having the authority to grant these privileges may revoke them. Although not true in all cases, privileges withheld normally are those that you have misused. For example, you may be denied use of the service club if you have been disorderly in the club, be denied government quarters if you have misused them, or lose on-post driving privileges if you commit a serious driving offense.

ADMONITIONS AND REPRIMANDS

The unit commander may give an oral or written admonition or reprimand for a specific act of misconduct. He submits a written admonition or reprimand in memorandum format to you for acknowledgment and rebuttal. The written admonition or reprimand may be filed in either the military personnel records jacket (MPRJ) (field 201 file) or official military personnel file (OMPF). Only a general officer or GCM convening authority (GCMCA) may direct that a written reprimand or admonition be filed in your OMPF. It is filed in your performance fiche until you successfully appeal it. (See AR 600-37.)

An admonition or reprimand that is filed in your MPRJ stays there until the soonest of the following occurs:

- You are transferred to another general court-martial (GCM) jurisdiction.
- The commander removes it.
- A maximum of three years has elapsed.
- You successfully appeal the reprimand.

ADMINISTRATIVE REDUCTIONS

The rank of enlisted soldiers may be reduced by court-martial. The rank of staff sergeants and below may also be reduced under UCMJ, Article 15. Commanders may administratively reduce your rank for inefficiency or civilian conviction. (See AR 600-200, Chapter 6.)

A company, battery, or separate detachment commander has the authority to reduce the rank of private through specialist or corporal. Field grade commanders of organizations authorized a lieutenant colonel or higher may reduce the rank of sergeant and staff sergeant. Commanders of organizations authorized a colonel or higher may reduce the rank of sergeant first class through command sergeant major. A commander may reduce corporals or specialists and below without convening a board to consider the case.

Commanders wanting to reduce the rank of sergeant through command sergeant major must first refer the case to a board of officers and enlisted soldiers for a hearing and recommendation. The exception is a mandatory reduction to private due to a serious civilian conviction. All board members must be senior in rank to the soldier under consideration. You may decline to appear before the board, or you may appear with an appointed or detailed judge advocate or with civilian counsel, at your own expense. You may request a non-lawyer military counsel if you wish. You may question the witnesses against you and present evidence in your own behalf. The commander may not take any action more severe than that the board recommends. Army regulations provide that if you have had your rank reduced due to inefficiency or due to conviction by civil court, you may appeal that reduction through command channels within 30 days.

Inefficiency

Commanders may evaluate you for inefficiency when your misconduct shows a lack of abilities or qualities expected of you. If you are an assigned soldier and have served in the same unit for at least 90 days, you may have your rank reduced by one pay grade for inefficiency.

Civilian Conviction

If you are sentenced to death or to confinement for one year or more and the sentence is not suspended, you will be reduced to private. If you are sentenced to confinement for more than 30 days but less than one year and the sentence is not suspended, you might have your rank reduced one or more pay grades. You might also have your rank reduced one or more pay grades for sentences less severe than those already mentioned. If you lose your rank, but your conviction by a civil court is reversed because of some error or irregularity, your rank will be restored. You may also be promoted if promotion was denied because of the reversed conviction. AR 600-200, Table 6-1, details administrative reduction based on a civilian conviction.

REVOCATION OF SECURITY CLEARANCE

Conduct that merits revocation or suspension of a security clearance includes criminal and immoral activities. Abuse of drugs and alcohol, excessive indebtedness, and repeated AWOL are grounds for such action. A clearance may also be denied or suspended if you are subject to coercion or undue influence, perhaps because you have a close relative living in a communist country.

If your commander receives information that may affect your clearance, he forwards it to the central personnel security clearance facility (CCF) for review to determine if it warrants clearance revocation. The commander may suspend your clearance pending results of the review. Before the CCF revokes the clearance, you will have an opportunity to reply in writing. If unsuccessful, you may appeal the revocation to Headquarters, Department of the Army.

BAR TO REENLISTMENT

You may be barred from reenlistment for deficiencies of character, conduct, attitude, proficiency, and/or motivation or for general undesirability for retention. These deficiencies often include the following:

- Tardiness for formations or duties.
- Being AWOL for 1 to 24 hours.
- Losses of clothing and equipment.
- Substandard personal appearance and hygiene.
- Persistent indebtedness.
- Frequent traffic violations.
- Recurrent punishments under UCMJ, Article 15.
- Use of sick call without medical justification.
- Tardiness in returning from pass or leave.
- Unwillingness to follow orders.
- Untrainability.
- Unadaptability to the military.
- Failure to manage personal affairs.
- Frequent difficulties with other soldiers.

The unit commander initiates a bar to reenlistment by summarizing in writing the grounds for such an action. You may then submit a statement in your own behalf. You have 7 days to prepare comments and collect evidence. The complete action is then forwarded to the authority who may approve or disapprove the bar.

An approved bar to reenlistment must be reviewed every 6 months and 30 days before your PCS or ETS. Bars may be removed at any time if you demonstrate your worthiness to be retained in the Army.

MOS RECLASSIFICATION

A unit commander must recommend reclassification of any awarded military occupational specialty (MOS) if UCMJ disciplinary action adversely affects your eligibility to perform duties in that MOS. Examples are a military policeman who commits an assault, a medical corpsman who is drunk while on duty, and a finance clerk who steals. The unit commander may recommend reclassification of any awarded MOS if you perform the duties of that MOS inadequately or attain unsatisfactory skill test scores.

CONDUCT OF INVESTIGATIONS

A commander may order investigations of many matters, such as the operation of the unit mess hall or the state of morale in the unit. The purpose of an investigation is to find out what happened, when it happened, where it happened, why it happened, and who was involved. Only after getting these facts should the commander decide what action to take.

Investigations might concern the loss of funds or equipment, damage to government property, disposition of the personal effects of deceased soldiers, or determination of whether you were injured in the line of duty. As a result of the latter, you could lose entitlement to disability retirement--

- If you were injured while AWOL.
- If the injury was due to your intentional misconduct, such as if you were shot while committing a robbery.
- If the injury was due to your willful neglect, such as if you were injured while driving intoxicated on the wrong side of the road.

Any time spent in the hospital would be classified lost time, and you would have to make it up at the end of your enlistment.

Unless the particular regulation governing the matter under investigation provides specific procedures, the board or investigating officer will follow the procedures in AR 15-6. Proceedings that involve a single investigating officer using informal procedures (see chapter 4) are designated investigations. Proceedings that involve a single investigating officer using formal procedures (see chapter 5) or more than one investigating officer using formal or informal procedures are designated a board of officers. The investigating officer must remain impartial during the investigation and must give the commander a complete picture of the matter as well as recommendations for the commander's action.

The boards conducting investigations will normally be composed of military personnel. You may be involved as a witness, a member of the board, an assistant to the board, or one of the persons whose conduct is under investigation.

RIGHTS OF SOLDIERS

When a board of officers is investigating your conduct or liability, you have some rights in relation to the board's hearing. This manual cannot state general rights because not every regulation provides the same procedures for investigations. Generally, you will receive some notice of the scope and purpose of the investigation. You will be allowed to submit evidence to the board and will be able to attend the board hearing. You will not have to testify before the board about any self-incriminating matter (UCMJ, Article 31). In most board proceedings, you may have a military counsel to help present your case and to question the witnesses. This counsel might be a lawyer, depending on the provisions of the regulation governing the hearing. You are normally allowed to hire a civilian counsel, but the Army will not pay for it. If under investigation, you should seek the advice of a legal officer.

LIMITED-USE POLICY

The limited-use policy is part of the Army's Alcohol and Drug Abuse Prevention and Control Program (ADAPCP). It prohibits the use of the following evidence against you in actions under the UCMJ or in characterizing separations:

- Mandatory urine or alcohol breath test results taken to determine your fitness for duty; taken to ascertain whether you need counseling, rehabilitation, or other medical treatment; or taken as part of your participation in the ADAPCP.
- Self-referral to ADAPCP. (Your volunteering for the program is protected information.)
- Admissions and other evidence that you voluntarily provide as part of your initial entry into ADAPCP. An example is illegal use or possession of drugs or alcohol before your initial referral to ADAPCP.
- Admissions, made in ADAPCP, to a physician or counselor at a scheduled interview concerning illegal use or possession of drugs or alcohol before your initial referral to ADAPCP.
- Evidence concerning illegal use or possession of drugs or alcohol obtained as a result of emergency medical care for drug or alcohol overdose, unless such treatment resulted from apprehension by military or civilian law enforcement officials. For example, if you are a drug user and have supplied a positive urinalysis as part of your participation in ADAPCP, the limited-use policy protects you from UCMJ action involving that urinalysis sample. If you are separated from the Army based in whole or in part on the positive urinalysis, you are entitled to an honorable discharge.

Each command has an alcohol and drug control officer who has information on the Alcohol and Drug Abuse Prevention and Control Program (ADAPCP). The ADAPCP offers treatment and rehabilitation to abusers who desire it and who demonstrate the potential to benefit from it. The limited-use policy does not legitimize use or possession of drugs-- it provides a way for you to admit your problems and get help. The policy is not to protect those who are trying to avoid disciplinary or adverse administrative actions.

The limited-use policy applies automatically; it cannot be withdrawn. If you have questions about the policy and its applications, consult your nearest staff judge advocate. The limited-use policy does not protect you in cases addressed in the following paragraphs.

PROSECUTION FOR OTHER OFFENSES

You may be prosecuted for offenses or misconduct other than prior use or personal possession of drugs, even though the misconduct may have occurred because of drug abuse. For example, you are not free from disciplinary or administrative actions for selling drugs to support your drug abuse.

PROSECUTION IN OTHER JURISDICTIONS

You may be tried by civilian courts for drug offenses for which you are free from prosecution by the military.

ADVERSE LINE-OF-DUTY DETERMINATIONS

You may lose pay and credit for accrued service time if you are unfit to perform duties for more than 24 hours because of alcohol or drug abuse. If you are hospitalized and medically unable to perform duty for more than 24 hours due to your own misconduct, you will lose pay only for the lost duty time. Hospitalization of less than 24 hours for drug or alcohol abuse does not apply. If you are placed in a drug or alcohol treatment facility, the time off duty will be recorded as an administrative absence.

OTHER SITUATIONS

The limited-use policy will not protect you from--

- Being investigated for criminal activity not directly related to drug use or possession.
- Losing your security clearance.
- Having your MOS reclassified or withdrawn.
- Having hazardous duty orders suspended or revoked.

COMPLAINT PROCESS

You can quickly and easily resolve most complaints by taking them to the first sergeant or the company commander. However, you will at times feel that an officer outside the company should handle the complaint. In these cases, you have several choices. In deciding which grievance procedure to follow and in making a complaint, you can get help from the local staff judge advocate office.

THE INSPECTOR GENERAL

Probably the best known person to receive and act on complaints is the inspector general (IG), who is present in every command. His job is to look into Army situations that may need correction. He also ensures, by inspecting equipment, procedures, and so forth, that the Army is following its own rules. The IG is chosen and trained to check complaints and has a direct line to everyone in the command, including the commanding general.

You may take complaints to the IG on any Army matters you think need correction or investigation. For example, you may complain that promotions are not fair. The IG must investigate all complaints. If complaints are valid, he takes them to the person who can solve them. If the IG finds that you do not have all the facts, he tries to explain the reasons for the situation to you. If the complaint involves something that cannot be solved at the local level, the IG sends it to a higher IG who can solve it--possibly all the way to the Inspector General of the Army.

ARTICLE 138 OF THE UCMJ

Article 138 of the UCMJ provides a complaint process for soldiers on active duty who think that they have been wronged by their commanding officers. A commanding officer is any commissioned officer authorized to impose non-judicial punishment under Article 15 of the UCMJ against the soldier. If asking the commander to correct the wrong does not resolve the complaint, you may make a formal complaint to any superior commissioned officer. The complaint must allege that the commander, in his line of duty, took some discretionary act (an act in which the commander had a lawful choice) that met one of the following criteria:

- It was beyond his authority.
- It was in violation of a law or regulation.
- It was arbitrary, capricious, or an abuse of discretion.
- It was materially unfair.

You must file the complaint within 90 days after learning of the wrong. The time the commander takes to consider your request is not part of the 90 days.

Any officer who receives a complaint must forward it to the officer who has authority to order a general court-martial for your command. The officer who is the general court martial convening authority (GCMCA) will investigate all allegations of the complaint and take action that he feels is proper. If you do not withdraw the complaint after the GCMCA takes his action, it is forwarded to The Judge Advocate General (TJAG). TJAG reviews the matter and takes final action on the complaint on behalf of the Secretary of the Army.

The Department of the Army policy is to resolve all grievances at the lowest level of command possible and to establish procedures quickly and fairly to resolve them. The complaint process under UCMJ, Article 138, is only one of these procedures. Some grievances can be handled more effectively under other procedures. Grievances not appropriate for a complaint under Article 138, for example, are those matters reviewable by a court-martial.

CIVIL RIGHTS LEGISLATION

A federal law prohibits motels, restaurants, theaters, and other places of entertainment from discriminating against you because of your race, color, religion, or national origin. Although this law does not prohibit sex discrimination, a business that discriminates against you because of sex violates DA policy. Other federal laws prohibit discrimination in the sale and rental of housing. Illegal discrimination occurs if you are denied a sale or rental due to your race, color, religion, national origin, or sex.

If you are a victim of discrimination, you can get help from one of several Army offices:

- The legal assistance office.
- The equal opportunity office.
- The IG.
- The housing referral office.

They will help you to file formal complaints of discrimination.

In making a complaint, you must sign a sworn statement about the incident. The Army then investigates the complaint. If the investigators discover discrimination, the local Army commander will try to stop it. If the business or landlord refuses to stop, your complaint may be sent to the US Attorney General for action, or you may file a formal complaint with a federal agency, with help from a legal assistance officer. You may also sue discriminating businesses or landlords in civil court.

MEMBERS OF CONGRESS

You may want to complain outside of the military. If you do, you can write any member of Congress about your complaint. The member of Congress then sends the complaint to the Department of the Army to validate it and to determine what the Army can do to solve it.

THE ARMED FORCES DISCIPLINARY CONTROL BOARD (AFDCB)

AR 190-24 governs the AFDCB. You may make complaints of unfair business practices and of any other conditions detrimental to your health, safety, or morale to this board. Examples of appropriate complaints are complaints of unsafe or unsanitary conditions in your apartment complex and of drug trafficking in an off-post bar. The AFDCB will investigate such complaints and try to remedy them. If the AFDCB verifies a complaint and cannot rectify the situations, the business may be made off-limits to you.

CHAPTER THREE

Military Justice

The rules of military justice stem from many sources. This chapter describes these sources; the roles of the commander, the staff judge advocate, the military judge, and the members of the court-martial; and the rights and procedures involved in non-judicial punishment.

SOURCES OF AUTHORITY

The rules governing military justice and military criminal law come from the following sources:

- **The Constitution of the United States.** The Constitution is the basic authority for the military criminal justice system in the United States Army. It allows Congress to make a separate military justice system.
- **The Uniform Code of Military Justice.** Congress enacted the Uniform Code of Military Justice (UCMJ) in 1950, thereby replacing the Articles of War from 1775. The UCMJ is a federal law that establishes our present system of military criminal justice. It describes what conduct is criminal and the types of courts and basic procedures used to process military criminal cases. The UCMJ is found in 10 United States Code, §§ 801-940 and in Appendix 2 of the Manual for Courts-Martial (MCM), United States, 1984.
- **The Manual for Courts-Martial (MCM), United States, 1984.** The MCM details the rules for military justice and has the force and effect of law. In passing the UCMJ, Congress gave power

to the President of the United States to establish military criminal procedures. The President did this by publishing the MCM. It explains military crimes, contains the rules of evidence, and sets forth rules for conducting courts-martial.

- **Army regulations.** The Secretary of the Army has authority to issue regulations, in addition to the UCMJ and MCM, that administrators of military justice must follow. For example, AR 27-10 covers the administration of military justice.

- **The United States Army Court of Military Review.** The Court of Military Review is the first appellate court in the military justice system. The court members are appellate military judges in the ranks of colonel and lieutenant colonel. In reviewing courts-martial convictions, the United States Army Court of Military Review issues written opinions, which are binding on Army courts-martial. A civilian, personally retained lawyer or an appellate defense counsel appointed by The Judge Advocate General may represent the accused.

- **The United States Court of Military Appeals.** The Court of Military Appeals is the highest appeals court within the military justice system. Effective 1 October 1990, it consists of five civilian judges appointed by the President of the United States. It is comparable in position and authority to a state supreme court and hears appeals on decisions of the United States Army Court of Military Review. It also issues written opinions containing rules on military justice. The Military Justice Act of 1983 allows decisions made by the Court of Military Appeals to be appealed to the United States Supreme Court.

- **The United States Supreme Court.** The Supreme Court is the highest court in the United States. It consists of nine justices whom the President appoints to life terms and the Senate confirms. It hears appeals from federal circuit courts, state supreme courts, and the Court of Military Appeals. The Supreme Court provides authoritative interpretations of the United States Constitution and usually hears only those cases that present significant legal issues.

MILITARY ROLES

The following paragraphs address the roles of the commander, the staff judge advocate, military judges, and court members in the military justice system.

THE COMMANDER

The unit (company, battery, troop, detachment, and so forth) commander is usually the first to learn of misconduct that might give rise to administrative action, non-judicial punishment, or court-martial charges. He must promptly investigate the circumstances of an alleged crime and decide what to do about it. In deciding what to do, the commander must consider the seriousness of the offense, your past record and your potential for further useful service, and the state of morale and discipline in the unit. He must decide whether to refer the matter up the chain of command or dispose of it within the unit by administrative action or by UCMJ, Article 15 (non-judicial punishment). If he forwards a case to a superior, that officer will apply the same criteria in deciding whether to take appropriate action or to forward the case still higher. Each commander is responsible for both enforcing the law and protecting your rights.

THE STAFF JUDGE ADVOCATE

The staff judge advocate (SJA) of the unit's division or post has a duty to see that criminal justice in the command is carried out properly and fairly. The SJA advises commanders at every level about their handling of cases. Judge advocates, all fully qualified lawyers, advise and represent soldiers accused of crimes. Although available through the office of the staff judge advocate, they are assigned to a separate organization, the United States Army Trial Defense Service (USATDS or TDS).

MILITARY JUDGES

Military judges are assigned to sit on all general and most special courts-martial. These individuals are experienced lawyers with training as military judges. They decide questions of law, instruct the court members on law that applies to the case, and ensure that the trial is conducted legally.

COURT MEMBERS

The commander selects active-duty soldiers to act as court members. An enlisted accused may request that enlisted soldiers hear his or her case. In such an instance, at least one-third of the members of the court will be enlisted. They may not, however, be from the same unit as the accused. All members of the court have an equal voice and vote. The accused has the right to challenge any member on the court, including the judge, if the member or judge is not impartial. The accused may also challenge one member of the court without reason. Any member successfully challenged takes no further part in the trial.

RIGHTS AND PROCEDURES

The following paragraphs address your rights as a soldier and the procedures that must be followed in the administration of military justice.

RIGHTS OF SOLDIERS

You have many basic rights under military criminal law, including--

- The right to a defense lawyer.
- The right to due process of law.
- The right to remain silent.
- Rights under the law of search and seizure.

Defense Lawyer

The Army provides a fully qualified military defense lawyer free of charge to any soldier facing special or general courts-martial. As your representative, the lawyer acts in your interest, advising and defending you to the best of his ability. Discussion about a case between you and your attorney is confidential under the attorney-client relationship. This means that the lawyer may not reveal what you have told him without your permission. If you are facing court-martial, you also have the right to have a civilian lawyer, but you must pay this cost or obtain the services without cost to the government. If you are not facing a special or general court-martial, you may still get advice from an Army lawyer on military criminal matters by contacting the local office of the staff judge advocate or Trial Defense Service office.

Due Process

Due process of the law provides that, at trial, you have the right to confront and cross examine all the witnesses against you. You also have the right to present evidence on your own behalf. You may not be found guilty of a crime until the government proves beyond a reasonable doubt that you committed the crime. A finding of guilty may be made only after a court has heard all the evidence relating to your guilt or innocence.

Remaining Silent

The UCMJ provides that if you are suspected of a crime, you may not be forced to speak against yourself. Before questioning, you must be advised of your right to remain silent. Also, if you are in custody, you must be told that you have the right to speak to a lawyer and have a lawyer present during questioning if you choose to answer questions.

Search and Seizure

The Fourth Amendment to the Constitution of the United States and the MCM govern examination of your person or property to discover and remove evidence. Military criminal law requires strict compliance with the Constitution and the MCM. Searches are permissible only under limited circumstances such as the following:

- **Search authorized by a commander.** A commander may order a search of your person or property when you are a member of his command. The decision to conduct a search, which may be reviewed by a court-martial, must be based upon probable cause.
- **Search incident to apprehension.** A person legally apprehending you may search you and your immediately available property. The property must be in your immediate control at the time of your apprehension.
- **Consent to search.** A search is lawful when made with your free and voluntary consent.
- **Search to prevent removal of criminal evidence.** If evidence of a crime is in danger of removal or destruction, and if time is not available to secure a commander's permission to search, a lawful search may be made.
- **Inspection for military readiness.** The commander has the authority to determine the military readiness of soldiers, organizations, and equipment. Evidence of a crime discovered during an authorized inspection may be seized and admitted as evidence at a court-martial.

PROCEDURES FOR COURT-MARTIAL

The Army's court-martial system includes--

- **Summary court-martial (SCM).** This type of court-martial is composed of one commissioned officer who tries minor crimes. The maximum punishment depends upon your rank but may not exceed confinement for one month, forfeiture of two-thirds pay for one month, and reduction in rank. You may consult a lawyer concerning the case, but you are not entitled to have an appointed military lawyer present at the trial. You have the right to refuse trial by SCM.
- **Special court-martial (SPCM).** An SPCM consists of at least three court members. The defense counsel must be a lawyer. A military judge is normally appointed for the trial. The maximum sentence is confinement for six months, forfeiture of two-thirds pay per month for six months, and reduction in rank to the lowest enlisted grade. In some instances, the sentence may include a bad-conduct discharge (BCD).
- **General court-martial (GCM).** A GCM tries the most serious offenses. It consists of at least five court members and a military judge. Both the prosecuting (trial) and defense counsel must be lawyers. A formal investigation must occur before the trial. The GCM judge may sentence you to any punishment authorized by law.

Just as in other American criminal courts, courts-martial are adversary proceedings. That is, the government and the accused each present matters that apply to their sides and must follow certain rules in doing so.

In either a general or a special court-martial with a military judge, you may choose to be tried by the military judge without the members. If the judge alone tries you, he decides if you are guilty or innocent. If the judge finds you guilty, he also determines your sentence. If members find you guilty, they determine your sentence.

You may plead guilty or not guilty. If you do not make a plea, the judge enters a plea of not guilty. Before trial, you may possibly agree to plead guilty in exchange for a promise by the convening authority to approve only a certain sentence. This is called a pretrial agreement.

The person who ordered each trial reviews its result. Either the Judge Advocate General or the Army Court of Military Review may also review the court-martial conviction, depending on the type of court-martial and the punishment imposed.

You may appeal certain convictions to the Court of Military Appeals, which consists of three civilian judges. The United States Supreme Court may review its decisions.

Appendix C shows the maximum imposable punishments for the different types of court martial.

PROCEDURES FOR ARTICLE 15

Under UCMJ, Article 15, you may be punished for minor offenses. The punishment is non-judicial because it is given by the commander instead of by a court-martial. If you are facing non-judicial punishment, you have rights and must make important decisions.

The commander may give non-judicial punishment only to soldiers under his command. Before punishing you under Article 15, the commander must make sure that--

- An offense was actually committed.
- The offense may be punished under the UCMJ.
- You committed the offense.
- Article 15 punishment is proper after considering the type of offense and your record.
- The proper type of non-judicial punishment, formal or summarized, is selected.

The commander must tell you, in writing, that he plans to give you a formal Article 15. He will notify you using DA Form 2627, advise you of your legal rights, and tell you where to find the lawyer's office. You must be given a reasonable amount of time to see a lawyer. You have the following rights:

- To refuse the Article 15 (unless attached to or embarked on a ship) and demand trial by court-martial.
- To know the type of offense committed.
- To have a public hearing.
- To have the help of a spokesperson.

- To present witnesses.
- To present matters in defense, extenuation, and mitigation.
- To examine documents or physical objects to be used against you.
- To say nothing.
- To appeal.

Written notification of a summarized Article 15 is not required. The commander will record the proceedings using a DA Form 2627-1. Only enlisted soldiers may receive summarized Article 15 punishment. The punishment is limited to 14 days' extra duty, 14 days' restriction, an oral admonition or reprimand, or any combination of these punishments. You must decide to accept or refuse a summarized Article 15 within 24 hours. You do not have a right to consult with a lawyer, bring a spokesperson to the hearing, or request an open hearing. You do receive notice of the nature of the offense and have the following rights:

- To present witnesses.
- To remain silent.
- To appeal.
- Unless attached to a ship, to refuse the summarized Article 15 and demand trial by court-martial.

Simply accepting the Article 15 procedure does not mean that you admit guilt. Rather, you agree to the use of the procedures of Article 15 to let the commander, instead of a court-martial, determine your guilt or innocence. If the commander determines that you are guilty, the type and amount of punishment the commander may impose under formal Article 15 procedures depends on his rank, your rank, and the size of the unit. (See Appendix C.)

A warrant officer, lieutenant, or captain may impose an Article 15 punishment. If a heavier punishment is warranted, the case may be sent to a field grade commander in the chain of command with a rank of major or above with a recommendation. The field grade commander may act on the recommendation or return the case to the lower commander for action. The superior commander, however, may not tell a subordinate commander when to give an Article 15 or how much punishment he should give.

A commander who gives an Article 15 has the power to grant you clemency. The commander may suspend your punishment for up to six months. The probation is an incentive to stay out of trouble. The original punishment is not effected unless the commander cancels your suspension due to further misconduct.

A commander may also reduce the amount or type of punishment when your conduct merits it. For example, he may reduce 14 days of extra duty to 10 days of restriction or 7 days of extra duty.

A commander may set aside a punishment when it is clear that the Article 15 should not have been given in the first place. You are then restored all your rights and privileges.

Every soldier who receives an Article 15 has the right to appeal. You may appeal if you believe that you are not guilty, if the commander did not follow the rules for giving an Article 15, or if the punishment is too severe. The commander who acts as the appellate authority normally is immediately superior to the commander who issued the Article 15. In other words, if a company commander issues the Article 15, the battalion commander will act as the appellate authority. An appellate authority may reject an appeal that is submitted more than 5 days after the commander imposes punishment.

In deciding what to do on appeal, the appellate commander may take any of the clemency actions discussed earlier to lessen the punishment; he may not, however, increase the punishment. The appellate commander must refer an Article 15 appeal to the SJA for a legal opinion if the Article 15 contains any of the following punishments:

- Arrest in quarters of more than 7 days.
- Correctional custody of more than 7 days.
- Forfeiture of more than 7 days' pay.
- Reduction in rank from a pay grade of E-4 and above.
- Extra duty of more than 14 days.
- Restriction of more than 14 days.

APPENDIX A

Sources of information and assistance table found on next page.

Sources of Information and Assistance

APPENDIX A

Numbers indicate order of contact.
X means as applicable.

	Squad/Sec Leader	Platoon Leader	First Sergeant	Company Commander	Unit Personnel Officer	Bn, Bde, Gp Commander	Chaplain¹	American Red Cross	Judge Advocate	Post Commander	Billeting Officer	School Superintendent	Inspector General	Finance Officer	Post Transportation Officer	Army Community Service
Appeals	1	2	3	4	X	X	X	X	X	X						
Assignment, reassignment, MOS, and proficiency pay	1	2	3	4	5	6	X			X			X			
Personnel matters, promotions, reduction, reenlistment, discharge, retirement, veteran's benefits	1	2	3	4	5	6				X		X				
Complaints	1	2	3	4	X	5	X		X	X	X	6	X	X		X
Debts and civilian creditors	1	2	3	4	X	X	X	X	X					X		X
Dependent schools	X	X	X	X					2		1	X				X
Family and religious affairs	X	X	X	X	X	X	X	X	X	X		X	X	X	X	X
Travel of dependents, shipment of cars and household goods			1	2	X	X		X	X	X			X	X	3	X
Medical service	1	2	3	4	5	X		X	X	X		X	X			X
Pay, allowances, incentive pay	1	2	3	4	5	7		X	X	X		X	6	X	X	X
Leave and passes	1	2	3	4	X	5						X	X			
Insurance, all types				X	X		X	X								
Legal assistance (US and foreign law), wills, powers of attorney						X		1	X							
Military schools	1	2	3	4	5	X				X		X				X
PX, commissary, QM sales store	1	2	3	X	X				X		X	X				X
Government quarters			1	2	3	X			X	X	X	X			X	
Registration and operation of POV			1	X	X	X		X	X	X		X				
Postal service			1	2	3					X		X				
Entry into US, passport, visa, naturalization, immigration			1	2	X	X	X	3	X				X			X
Home conditions, emergency leave	1	2	3	4	6	7	X	5	X				X	X	X	X
Emergency financial assistance	1	2	3	4	5	X	X						X	X	6	6

¹The chaplain is always available; the telephone number is posted in the orderly room.

APPENDIX B

Discharge Benefits charts

This chart shows eligibility for benefits based on type of discharge. It does not indicate the other requirements that must be met.

Legend
E—eligible
NE—not eligible
Off—officers
ENL—enlisted
TBD—to be determined by the administering agency

Discharge Benefits

APPENDIX B

This chart shows eligibility for benefits based on type of discharge. It does not indicate the other requirements that must be met.

Legend
E—eligible
NE—not eligible
Off—officers
ENL—enlisted
TBD—to be determined by the administering agency

BENEFITS ADMINISTERED BY THE ARMY	HONORABLE Off and ENL: DD Form 256A	GENERAL Off and ENL: DD Form 257A (Under Honorable Conditions)	UNDER OTHER THAN HONORABLE CONDITIONS [7]	BAD CONDUCT (Under Other Than Honorable Conditions)	DISHONORABLE (General Court-Martial) (including Dismissal of an Officer) [2]
Payment for accrued leave	E	E	NE	NE	NE
Death gratuity (6 months' pay) and other death benefits [3]	E	E	E	E	NE
Transportation home	E	E	E	E	E
Transportation of dependents and household goods home	E	E	TBD[4]	TBD[4]	TBD[4]
Wearing of military uniform	E	E	NE	NE	NE
Admission to soldiers' home [5]	E	E	NE	NE	NE
Army Board for Correction of Military Records	E	E	E	E	E
Army Discharge Review Board	E	E	E	NE[6]	NE
Burial in Army national cemeteries	E	E	NE	NE	NE
Burial in Army post cemeteries [7]	E	E	NE	NE	NE

[1] This discharge category includes the discharge of officers under other than honorable conditions, AR 635-100, para 1-4c.

[2] An officer who resigns for the good of the service (usually to avoid court-martial charges) will be ineligible for benefits administered by the Veterans Administration, 38 USC 3103; the Department of Labor, unemployment compensation only, 5 USC 8521; and the Social Security Administration, Old Age and Disability Insurance, SSA Handbook.

[3] Those discharged from enlisted status while patients in US hospitals and who continue to be patients until the date of death and those who die as military prisoners are entitled to recovery care, disposition of remains, and expenses incident to death 10 USC 1481-1482.

[4] Soldiers separated or discharged under other than honorable conditions whose sentence was approved by the convening authority before 1 Sep 87 are not eligible. The installation order issuing authority determines if dependent travel and household goods shipment are in the best interests of the Army. JFTR, paras U5240J and M53703.

[5] The statute provides that veterans must have served "honestly and faithfully" for 20 years or been disabled; it excludes convicted felons, deserters, mutineers, or habitual drunkards unless rehabilitated.

[6] Under 10 USC 1533(e), if their BCDs were given by a general court-martial, former soldiers are not eligible for this benefit. The Code is silent if the discharge was given by a special court-martial.

[7] Only if an immediate relative is buried in the cemetery.

Discharge Benefits

CONTINUED

BENEFITS ADMINISTERED BY THE VETERANS ADMINISTRATION[3]	HONORABLE (Off and Enl: DD Form 256A)	GENERAL (Off and Enl: DD Form 257A) (Under Honorable Conditions)	UNDER OTHER THAN HONORABLE CONDITIONS[1][2]	BAD CONDUCT (Under Other Than Honorable Conditions)	DISHONORABLE (General Court-Martial) (Including Dismissal of an Officer)[3]
Dependency and indemnity compensation	E	E	TBD	TBD	NE
Pension for nonservice-connected disability or death	E	E	TBD	TBD	NE
Medal of Honor Roll pension	E	E	TBD	TBD	NE
Insurance	E	E	TBD[4]	TBD[4]	TBD[4]
Vocational rehabilitation (DV)	E	E	TBD	TBD	NE
Educational assistance (including flight training and apprentice training)	E	E	TBD	TBD	NE
Survivors' and dependents' educational assistance	E	E	TBD	TBD	NE
Home and other loans	E	E	TBD	TBD	NE
Hospitalization and domiciliary care	E	E	TBD	TBD	NE
Medical and dental services	E	E	TBD	TBD	NE
Prosthetic appliances (DV)	E	E	TBD	TBD	NE
Guide dogs and equipment for blindness (DV)	E	E	TBD	TBD	NE
Special housing (DV)	E	E	TBD	TBD	NE
Automobiles (DV)	E	E	TBD	TBD	NE
Funeral and burial expenses	E	E	TBD	TBD	NE
Burial flag	E	E	TBD	TBD	NE
Burial in national cemetery	E	E	TBD	TBD	NE
Headstone marker	E	E	TBD	TBD	NE

[1] This discharge category includes the discharge of officers under other than honorable conditions, AR 635-100, para 1.4c.

[2] Officers who resign for the good of the service (usually to avoid court martial charges) will be ineligible for benefits administered by the Veterans Administration, 38 USC 3103; the Department of Labor, unemployment compensation only, 5 USC 8521; and the Social Security Administration, Old Age and Disability Insurance, SSA Handbook.

[3] Benefits from the Veterans Administration are not payable to—
- Persons discharged as conscientious objectors who refused to perform military duty or refused to wear the uniform or otherwise comply with lawful orders of competent military authority.
- Persons who have been discharged for a sentence of a general court-martial.
- Officers who have resigned for the good of the service.
- Deserters.
- Aliens with specific exemptions during a period of hostilities, 38 USC 3103.
- Those discharged by acceptance of other than honorable discharges to avoid court martial; mutiny or spying; felony offenses involving moral turpitude; willful and persistent misconduct; or homosexual acts involving aggravating circumstances or other factors

[4] Any persons who are guilty of mutiny, treason, spying, or desertion or who, because of conscientious objections, refuse to serve in the armed forces or to wear the uniform shall forfeit all rights to National Service Life Insurance and Serviceman's Group Life Insurance, 38 USC 711, 773.

Discharge Benefits

CONTINUED

> This chart shows eligibility for benefits based on type of discharge. It does not indicate the other requirements that must be met.
>
> **Legend**
> E— eligible
> NE— not eligible
> Off— officers
> ENL— enlisted
> TBD— to be determined by the administering agency

BENEFITS ADMINISTERED BY OTHER FEDERAL AGENCIES	HONORABLE OH and ENL: DD Form 256A	GENERAL OH and ENL: DD Form 257A (Under Honorable Conditions)	UNDER OTHER THAN HONORABLE¹ ² CONDITIONS (Under Other than Honorable Conditions)	BAD CONDUCT (Under Other than Honorable Conditions)	DISHONORABLE (General Court-Martial) (including Dismissal of an Officer)²
Preference for farm loans (Dept of Agriculture)	E	E	E	E	NE
Preference for farm and other rural housing loans (Dept of Agriculture)	E	E	E	E	NE
Civil service preference (OPM)	E	E	NE	NE	NE
Civil service retirement credit (OPM)	NE	NE	NE	NE	NE
Reemployment rights (Dept of Labor)	E	E	E	E	NE
Job counseling and employment and training placement through state job services (Dept of Labor)	E	E	E	E	NE
Unemployment compensation for ex-soldiers² (Dept of Labor)	E	TBD	NE	NE	NE
Naturalization benefits (Dept of Justice) (INS)	E	E	NE	NE	NE
Old age survivors and disability insurance (SSA)	E	E	TBD	TBD³	NE
Job preference, public works projects (Dept of Commerce)⁴	E	E	TBD	TBD	NE

¹This discharge category includes the discharge of officers under other than honorable conditions, AR 635-100, para 1-4c.

²Officers who resign for the good of the service (usually to avoid court-martial charges) will be eligible for Department of Labor unemployment compensation only, 5 USC 8521, and Social Security Administration, Old Age and Disability Insurance, SSA Handbook. In cases where the soldiers have pre-1957 service, they are eligible for pre-1957 military wage credits. While the type of discharge does not affect post-1957 Social Security benefits, entitlement to the pre-1957 wage credit may be affected by the type of discharge.

³NE if BCD was given by a general court-martial, SSA Handbook.

⁴Disabled veterans and Vietnam era veterans only. General eligibility: The eligibility of benefits set forth are not the sole determining factors but only list the effect of the various types of discharge. The states also provide various benefits that will be influenced by the type of discharge, but information on state benefits should be obtained from state agencies.

APPENDIX C

Maximum Imposable Punishments for Enlisted Soldiers on next page.

Maximum Imposable Punishments
(Enlisted Soldiers)

APPENDIX C

Legend
NA—not applicable

	Punitive Discharge	Confinement	Hard Labor Without Confinement	Correctional Custody	Restriction	Extra Duties	Reduction in Rank	Forfeiture of Pay	Fine	Admonition or Reprimand
Article 15, UCMJ: imposed by CPT or below	No	No	No	7 days; E-3 and below	14 days	14 days	To one grade lower (if commander can promote to present grade)	7 days	No	Yes
Article 15, UCMJ: imposed by MAJ or above	No	No	No	30 days; E-3 and below	60 days	45 days	E-4 and below, to lowest grade; E-5 and E-6, one grade lower (if commander can promote to present grade)	½ pay per month for 2 months	No	Yes
Summarized Article 15, UCMJ	No	No	No	No	14 days	14 days	No	No	No	Yes
Summary court-martial	No	1 month; no if E-5 or above	45 days; no if E-5 or above	No	2 months	NA	To lowest grade; E-5 or above, to one grade lower	2/3 pay for 1 month	Not in excess of 2/3 pay for 1 month	Yes
Special court-martial	BCD if designated	6 months	3 months	No	2 months	NA	To lowest grade	2/3 pay for 6 months	Not in excess of 2/3 pay for 6 months	Yes
General court-martial	DD or BCD	Depends on offense¹	3 months	No	2 months	NA	To lowest grade	Total forfeiture (length of time depends on offense)	Yes	Yes

¹No punishment can exceed that designated by Congress as the maximum punishment for the specific offense. See specific offenses in the MCM, Part IV.

GLOSSARY

ABCMR Army Board for Correction of Military Records

ADAPCP Alcohol and Drug Abuse Prevention and Control Program

Admonition A warning or reminder not to repeat certain misconduct.

ADRB Army Discharge Review Board

AFDCB Armed Forces Disciplinary Control Board

Appellate Court A court that has the authority to review the judgement of another.

AR Army regulation

ATTN attention

AWOL absent without leave

BCD bad-conduct discharge

bde brigade

bn battalion

CCF central (personnel security) clearance facility

co company

DA Department of the Army

DC District of Columbia

DOD Department of Defense

Due Process of Law The premise that a soldier must be considered innocent until proven guilty at a trial by legal and competent evidence.

ETS expiration term of service

FM field manual

GCM general court-martial

GCMCA general court-martial convening authority

Gratuities free gifts

IG inspector general

JTR Joint Travel Regulation

MCM Manual for Courts-Martial

MOS military occupational specialty

MPRJ military personnel records jacket

OMPF official military personnel file

OPM Office of Personnel Management

PCS permanent change of station

Power of Attorney A legal document that authorizes one person to act on behalf of another.

REFRAD release from active duty

Remission Cancellation of any punishments that have not been served.

Reprimand A formal act of scolding an offender for misconduct.

SCM summary court-martial

sec leader section leader

SJA staff judge advocate

SP4 specialist fourth class

SPCM special court-martial

SSA Social Security Administration

SSCRA Soldiers' and Sailors' Civil Relief Act

TDS (United States Army) Trial Defense Service

TJAG The Judge Advocate General

UCMJ Uniform Code of Military Justice

Underground Newspaper A newspaper published to express criticism against the United States, the military, or its officials.

US United States

USATDS United States Army Trial Defense Service

USC United States Code

Will A legal document that ensures that when someone dies, his property will go to whomever he specifies. A will also permits parents to nominate guardians for their minor children in the event of the deaths of both parents.

REFERENCES

SOURCES USED

These are the sources quoted or paraphrased in this publication.

AR 15-6 Procedures for Investigating Officers and Board of Officers. 11 May 1988.

AR 20-1 Inspector General Activities and Procedures. 15 December 1989.

AR 27-3 Legal Assistance. 11 March 1989.

AR 27-10 Military Justice. 22 December 1989.

AR 27-20 Claims. 28 February 1990.

AR 210-7 Commercial Solicitation on Army Installations. 15 December 1978.

AR 600-15 Indebtedness of Military Personnel. 19 March 1986.

AR 600-8-2 Suspension of Favorable Personnel Actions (Flags). 1 March 1988.

AR 600-50 Standards of Conduct for Department of the Army Personnel. 28 January 1988.

AR 600-85 Alcohol and Drug Abuse Prevention and Control Program. 27 April 1988.

AR 630-5 Leave and Passes. 1 July 1984.

AR 635-200 Enlisted Personnel. 1 December 1988.

AR 930-4 Army Emergency Relief. 1 April 1985.

Constitution of the United States

Misc Pub 8-1 Joint Federal Travel Regulation.

Misc Pub 9-2 Manual for Courts-Martial, United States. 1984.

United States Code (U.S.C.)

DOCUMENTS NEEDED

These documents must be available to the intended users of this publication.

DA Form 2028 Recommended Changes to Publications and Blank Forms.

DA Form 2627 Record of Proceedings Under Article 15, UCMJ.

DA Form 2627-1 Summarized Record of Proceedings Under Article 15, UCMJ.

DD Form 256A Honorable Discharge Certificate.

DD Form 257A General Discharge Certificate (Under Honorable Conditions).

READINGS RECOMMENDED

These readings contain relevant supplemental information.

AR 15-130 Army Clemency Board.

AR 15-180 Army Discharge Review Board.

AR 15-185 Army Board for Correction of Military Records.

AR 27-1 Judge Advocate Legal Service.

AR 27-40 Litigation.

AR 27-50 Status of Forces Policies, Procedures, and Information.

AR 27-55 Authority of Armed Forces Personnel to Perform Notarial Acts.

AR 190-22 Searches, Seizures and Disposition of Property.

AR 190-24 Armed Forces Disciplinary Control Boards and Off-Installation Military Enforcement.

AR 195-2 Criminal Investigation Activities.

AR 195-5 Evidence Procedures.

AR 210-1 Private Organizations on Department of the Army Installations.

AR 210-51 Army Housing Referral Service Program.

AR 340-21 The Army Privacy Program.

AR 350-30 Code of Conduct/Survival, Evasion, Resistance and Escape (SERE) Training.

AR 360-5 Army Public Affairs, Public Information.

AR 360-61 Community Relations.

AR 380-53 Communications Security Monitoring.

AR 405-16 Homeowner's Assistance Program.

AR 405-20 Federal Legislative Jurisdiction.

AR 600-4 Remission or Cancellation of Indebtedness--Enlisted Members.

AR 600-9 The Army Weight Control Program.

AR 600-20 Army Command Policy.

AR 600-37 Unfavorable Information.

AR 600-40 Apprehension, Restraint, and Release to Civil Authorities.

AR 600-43 Conscientious Objection.

AR 600-240 Marriage in Oversea Commands.

AR 600-290 Passports and Visas.

AR 601-280 Total Army Retention Program.

AR 608-3 Naturalization and Citizenship of Military Personnel and Dependents.

AR 608-8 Mortgage Insurance for Service Members.

AR 608-9 The Survivor Benefit Plan.

AR 608-61 Application for Authorization to Marry Outside of the United States.

AR 608-99 Family Support, Child Custody, and Paternity.

AR 623-105 Officer Evaluation Reporting System.

AR 623-205 Enlisted Evaluation Reporting System.

AR 630-10 Absence Without Leave and Desertion.

AR 633-30 Military Sentences to Confinement.

AR 635-40 Physical Evaluation for Retention, Retirement or Separation.

AR 635-100 Officer Personnel.

AR 635-120 Officer Resignations and Discharges.

AR 930-5 American National Red Cross Service Program and Army Utilization.

DA Pam 25-30 Consolidated Index of Army Publications and Blank Forms.

DA Pam 25-51 The Army Privacy Program-System Notices and Exemption Rules.

By Order of the Secretary of the Army:

CARL E. VUONO

General, United States Army

Chief of Staff

Official:

PATRICIA P. HICKERSON

Colonel, United States Army

The Adjutant General

DISTRIBUTION:

Active Army, USAR, and ARNG: To be distributed in accordance with DA Form 12-11E, requirements for FM 27-14, Legal Guide for Soldiers (Qty rqr block no. 1090)

www.ingramcontent.com/pod-product-compliance
Lightning Source LLC
Chambersburg PA
CBHW081613170526
45166CB00009B/2949